PHOTOGRAPHY BY RICHARD EXLEY
EDITED BY HELEN EXLEY

Dedicated to Katalin Merczel. Thank you for the support that you have shown towards our company. And, especially for your strength and help during the Covid 19 crisis, we could not have produced this or any of our other recent books without you.

Published in 2020 by Helen Exley®LONDON in Great Britain.
All the words by Stuart and Linda Macfarlane, Linda Macfarlane, Stuart Macfarlane, Brian Clyde, Amanda Bell, Pamela Dugdale, Dalton Exley, Charlotte Gray, Hannah C. Klein, Odile Dormeuil, Linda Gibson, Helen Exley, Pam Brown, Margot Thomson, Mathilde Forestier, Mathilde & Sébastien Forestier are copyright © Helen Exley Creative Ltd 2020.
Photography by Richard Exley © Helen Exley Creative Ltd 2020.
Design, selection and arrangement by Helen Exley © Helen Exley Creative Ltd 2020.

ISBN: 978-1-78485-316-7

12 11 10 9 8 7 6 5 4 3 2 1

Do more of what makes you happy...

Write it on your heart that every day
is the best day of the year.

RALPH WALDO EMERSON

If you love this book…
you will probably want to know how to find
other Helen Exley® books like it.
They're all listed on

www.helenexley.com

MIX
Paper from
responsible sources
FSC® C081635

Helen Exley® LONDON
16 Chalk Hill, Watford, Hertfordshire, WD19 4BG, UK
www.helenexley.com

You can follow us on 🅕 and 🅞

Do more of what makes you happy...

JANUARY 2

Surround yourself with only people
who are going to lift you higher.

OPRAH WINFREY

Do more of what makes you happy...

Think of all the beauty that's
still left in and around you and be happy!

ANNE FRANK

Do more of what makes you happy...

JANUARY 3

The best things are nearest: breath in your nostrils, light in your eyes, flowers at your feet, duties at your hand, the path of Right just before you. Do not grasp at the stars, but do life's plain common work as it comes, certain that daily duties and daily bread are the sweetest things in life.

ROBERT LOUIS STEVENSON

Do more of what makes you happy...

DECEMBER 30

It's not so much about getting everything
you want and about how much you have,
it's more about how little it takes you
to feel content, to be happy. It's so much less
than people think it is. It's a lightness.
A letting go, a release into eternity. It's a freeing up,
a release of tensions. It's actually
easier, far, far easier. It's right under your nose.

DALTON EXLEY

Do more of what makes you happy...

JANUARY 4

Each day, as you awake, give thanks
that you are alive. Give thanks that you are who you are,
while accepting that you are not perfect.
Make a commitment to yourself that you will give purpose
to the day ahead – this beautiful day of your life. Then,
whatever you choose to do, do it
with determination and with a smile on your face.
Enjoy this day of your life.

STUART & LINDA MACFARLANE

Do more of what makes you happy...

DECEMBER 29

The longer I live, the more apparent
it becomes to me that paradise is
not a goal at the end of the road, but the road itself.

DOLLY PARTON

Do more of what makes you happy...

JANUARY 5

Happiness is not something
you find, like a gold coin
in the mud.
It is something you make
by how you live your life.
It's made from how you act,
your kindness, your care,
your thoughtfulness, your
unselfishness, your love.

DALTON EXLEY

Do more of what makes you happy...

DECEMBER 28

Did I offer peace today?
Did I bring a smile to someone's face?
Did I say words of healing?
Did I let go of my anger and resentment?
Did I forgive? Did I love? These are the real questions.
I must trust that the little bit of love that
I sow now will bear many fruits.

HENRI J. NOUWEN

Do more of what makes you happy...

Increase your happy times, letting yourself go;
follow your desire and best advantage.
And "do your thing" while you are still on this earth,
According to the command of your heart.

AFRICAN PROVERB

Do more of what makes you happy...

DECEMBER 27

There are only two ways to live your life.
One is as though nothing is a miracle.
The other is as though everything is a miracle.

ALBERT EINSTEIN

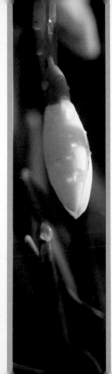

Do more of what makes you happy...

JANUARY 7

Here's a life.
Untouched pages stretching ahead.
What will you do with them?
What will you write?
Forget the ink blots on the past.
The aimless scribblings.
The scratched out mistakes.
This is all new, clear, waiting.
Take a deep breath. Begin.

PAM BROWN

Do more of what makes you happy...

DECEMBER 26

I move through my day-to-day life with
a sense of appreciation and gratitude that comes
from knowing how fortunate I truly am and how
unearned all that I am thankful for really is.
To have this perspective in my everyday consciousness
is in itself a gift, for it leads to
feeling "graced", or blessed, each time.

JEAN SHINODA BOLEN

Do more of what makes you happy...

JANUARY 8

Happiness is wanting your past, present and future
just the way it is, was and always will be.
Not wishing for the other.

BLACKWOLF (ROBERT JONES), OJIBWE, AND GINA JONES

Do more of what makes you happy...

DECEMBER 25

There is no happiness more precious than the giving and receiving of love. Nurture the love of those dear to you. Keep it bright and perfect. Never forget that love is the biggest blessing in your life.

STUART & LINDA MACFARLANE

Do more of what makes you happy...

When we value material things more than we value
the well-being of mankind, the door to the heart
is closed. When we are decent to others
and share ourselves through kindness and compassion,
the door to the heart is open.
The greatest truth in life is that the happiness
and peace of each can be reached only through
the happiness and peace of all.

MUHAMMAD ALI

Do more of what makes you happy...

DECEMBER 24

Life engenders life. Energy creates energy. It is by spending oneself that one becomes rich.

SARAH BERNHARDT

Do more of what makes you happy...

JANUARY 10

In the woods
I am blessed.
Happy is everyone
in the woods.
What glory
in the woodland.

LUDWIG VAN BEETHOVEN

Do more of what makes you happy...

DECEMBER 23

Be the decision maker.
The ideas person.
The person that gets things done.
You may not make the best decision
on every occasion but that is fine.
What is important is that
you have a vision and find a way
of achieving it.

LINDA GIBSON

Do more of what makes you happy...

It is easy to hold a grudge against a person
that you believe has wronged you – all too easy.
It is harder, much, much harder to forgive
that person. But when you hold a grudge
the main person to suffer is you. However,
when you forgive someone, you cleanse yourself of
resentment. You free your heart from anger
and bitterness. You can smile again.

MATHILDE FORESTIER

Do more of what makes you happy...

To be content with what we possess is the greatest and most secure of riches.

MARCUS TULLIUS CICERO

Do more of what makes you happy...

When you finally allow yourself
to trust joy and embrace it,
you will find you dance with everything.

EMMANUEL

Do more of what makes you happy...

DECEMBER 21

HAPPINESS IS A QUIET, PERPETUAL REJOICING IN SMALL EVENTS.

PAM BROWN

Do more of what makes you happy...

JANUARY 13

The Japanese practice of Shinrin Yoku, or Forest Bathing,
is a way of de-stressing and getting a sense of well-being
by spending time immersed in a forest setting.
Walk along a quiet forest path. Sit for a while and do nothing but
appreciate your surroundings. Take in all the sights
and sounds and smells. Let yourself relax fully and forget
any worries that you may have. Forest Bathing draws
on the therapeutic powers of nature and helps to connect you
with the natural environment. Why not give it a try?

STUART MACFARLANE

Do more of what makes you happy...

DECEMBER 20

Happiness is a rare plant, that seldom
takes root on earth: few ever enjoy it,
except for a brief period; the search
after it is rarely rewarded by the discovery.
But, there is an admirable substitute for it,
which all may hope to attain,
as its attainment depends wholly on self —
and that is, a contented spirit.

LADY MARGUERITE BLESSINGTON

Do more of what makes you happy...

Don't hurry,
don't worry.
You're only here
for a short visit.
So be sure
to stop and smell
the flowers.

WALTER HAGAN

Do more of what makes you happy...

DECEMBER 19

If you think something
is missing in your life
or you're not getting what
you deserve, remember
that there's no
Yellow Brick Road
to happiness. You lead life;
it doesn't lead you.

OPRAH WINFREY

Do more of what makes you happy...

JANUARY 15

In our lives, change
is unavoidable,
loss is unavoidable.
In the adaptability
and ease with which
we experience change,
lies our happiness
and freedom.

GAUTAMA BUDDHA

Do more of what makes you happy...

We act as though comfort and luxury were the chief requirements of life, when all that we need to make us really happy is something to be enthusiastic about.

CHARLES KINGSLEY

Do more of what makes you happy...

Make the decision right now to take thirty minutes of exercise each day and to eat a little more healthily. It may feel inconvenient at the moment but your future self will truly thank you for making the sacrifice. A healthy, happy future is within your gift.

STUART & LINDA MACFARLANE

Do more of what makes you happy...

DECEMBER 17

Carefully consider how you wish to live your life;
what principles you wish to follow.
Now consider how you currently live your life.
Understand the gap between the two and take
measures to close that gap. Often the reason that
we fail to live as we should is because we
have not taken time to consider what we want.
Do not make that mistake.

STUART & LINDA MACFARLANE

Do more of what makes you happy...

JANUARY 17

Pause and think about,
and even write down, five things
you are good at. Write down
ten things in your life you are truly
grateful for. Research shows
just actually doing this small exercise
can increase your happiness
by twenty-five per cent.

DALTON EXLEY

Do more of what makes you happy...

DECEMBER 16

Of all forms of caution, caution in love
is perhaps the most fatal to true happiness.

BERTRAND RUSSELL

Do more of what makes you happy...

JANUARY 18

A vigorous five-mile walk will do more good
for an unhappy but otherwise healthy adult
than all the medicine and psychology in the world.

PAUL DUDLEY WHITE

Do more of what makes you happy...

DECEMBER 15

Digging in the garden on a fine spring morning
gives as great a happiness
as sailing on a millionaire's yacht.

PAM BROWN

Do more of what makes you happy...

JANUARY 19

Find kind, gentle friends. Find fun friends to share free, happy days. Enjoy being with them. May there always be friends to share your laughter, your troubles and your victories.

HANNAH C. KLEIN

Do more of what makes you happy...

DECEMBER 14

LAUGHING
MAKES
EVERYTHING
EASIER.

CARMEN ELECTRA

Do more of what makes you happy...

JANUARY 20

One thing I know:
the only ones among you who will be really happy
are those who
will have sought and found how to serve.

ALBERT SCHWEITZER

Do more of what makes you happy...

Our capacity to draw happiness from
aesthetic objects or material goods in fact seems
critically dependent on our first satisfying
a more important range of emotional or psychological
needs, among them the need for understanding,
for love, expression and respect.

ALAIN DE BOTTON

Do more of what makes you happy...

Praise and blame, gain and loss,
pleasure and sorrow come and go
like the wind. To be happy,
rest like a great tree in the midst of them all.

GAUTAMA BUDDHA

Do more of what makes you happy...

DECEMBER 12

Be astounded by the great things in life —
but take time to notice the small
astonishments half hidden in the grass.

PAMELA DUGDALE

Do more of what makes you happy…

JANUARY 22

To stand back and look at something
one has done and be proud of its perfection
— that's HAPPINESS.

ODILE DORMEUIL

Do more of what makes you happy...

DECEMBER 11

WHAT SUNSHINE IS TO FLOWERS, SMILES ARE TO HUMANITY.

JOSEPH ADDISON

Do more of what makes you happy...

JANUARY 23

The happiest excitement in life is to be convinced that one is fighting for all one is worth on behalf of some clearly seen and deeply felt good.

RUTH BENEDICT

Do more of what makes you happy...

DECEMBER 10

The greatest determiner
of human happiness
is whether or not we have
someone to love and confide in.

DR. JOYCE BROTHERS

Do more of what makes you happy...

JANUARY 24

Be still.
Find happiness
in silence.

PAM BROWN

Do more of what makes you happy...

DECEMBER 9

KEEP A GREEN TREE IN OUR HEART AND PERHAPS A SINGING BIRD WILL COME.

CHINESE PROVERB

Do more of what makes you happy...

How simple
and frugal a thing
is happiness...
All that is required
to feel that here
and now is happiness
is a simple, frugal heart.

NIKOS KAZANTZAKIS

Do more of what makes you happy...

Never stop learning. Seek knowledge on
a diverse range of subjects. Be happy.

MATHILDE FORESTIER

Do more of what makes you happy...

JANUARY 26

Switch off the irritation
of the television.
Switch off the stressful
distraction of the phone.
Sit comfortably
and stare at a flower.
Just you and the flower.
Beauty. Peace. Simplicity.
Perfection.
This is life as it should be.

LINDA GIBSON

Do more of what makes you happy...

DECEMBER 7

Mindfulness is a natural ability that we all possess
but rarely use. Simply, it is the practice of freeing
our minds from the torrent of distractions
that constantly bombard us. It is about enjoying
and making the most of this present moment
instead of lamenting over the past or worrying about
what the future holds. It is about calmly and purposefully
making today a focus for fun.

STUART & LINDA MACFARLANE

Do more of what makes you happy...

Studies have shown that Mindfulness Meditation helps reduce stress, helps improve sleep and makes us feel more positive. Rather than being negatively concerned about past or future events Mindfulness Meditation helps us focus on the present – to "Live in the Moment". The great thing is that the exercises can be practised in spare moments such as while you shower, while washing the dishes or even on a boring journey.

STUART & LINDA MACFARLANE

Do more of what makes you happy...

DECEMBER 6

The only true happiness comes from squandering ourselves for a purpose.

JOHN MASON BROWN

Do more of what makes you happy...

ONE LONELY PERSON.
ONE OTHER
LONELY PERSON.
ONE SHY SMILE,
ONE FRIENDLY GRIN.
TWO HAPPY PEOPLE.

HELEN EXLEY

Do more of what makes you happy...

LAUGHING
CHEERFULNESS
THROWS
SUNLIGHT
ON ALL THE PATHS
OF LIFE.

JEAN PAUL RICHTER

Do more of what makes you happy...

A smile is an indication
of a happy heart,
and when you smile it
changes
your perception.
It can create
a better day.

GOLDIE HAWN

Do more of what makes you happy...

DECEMBER 4

Be kind to everyone you meet. Look less at what you don't like about people and more about what you can like about them. Love and care for those you love. You will be needed, you will be wanted and you will be loved. You will be helping spread that happiness — and you will find that happiness.

DALTON EXLEY

Do more of what makes you happy...

JANUARY 30

Happiness is infectious. Spread it with joy.

PAM BROWN

Do more of what makes you happy...

Quieten your mind
and close your eyes.
Be still and feel
the sun upon your face.
Hear the shrill of bird song.
Rejoice in your senses.
Rejoice in life.

PAM BROWN

Do more of what makes you happy...

Never lose an
opportunity
of seeing anything that
is beautiful... Welcome
beauty in every fair face,
in every fair sky,
in every flower...

RALPH WALDO EMERSON

Do more of what makes you happy...

A smile creates
sunshine
in the home...
fosters goodwill
in business...
and is the best
antidote for trouble.

AUTHOR UNKNOWN

Do more of what makes you happy...

FEBRUARY 1

Hold happiness as you would a butterfly –
softly, gently – enchanted by the moment
– accepting that it must pass.

PAM BROWN

Do more of what makes you happy...

DECEMBER 1

When you are feeling overwhelmed
it is important to set yourself small goals rather
than thinking about the daunting number of things
that are demanding your attention. On these occasions
getting showered and then having breakfast
may be satisfactory accomplishments.
Give yourself time to be proud of these small
steps before setting yourself your next task.

LINDA GIBSON

Do more of what makes you happy...

FEBRUARY 2

Stop for a moment during the day and let the sun
bathe your face. Take a second or two to listen to
the music of the laughter of your children as they play.
Go to a river bank and
listen to the sound of the water,
the chirping birds, the blowing of the wind.
It is the world around you that speaks to you,
that will inspire you. If you listen hard enough,
you will find the voice within yourself, and the ability
and the power to make a difference.

ERIN BROCKOVICH

Do more of what makes you happy...

NOVEMBER 30

Love and joy are twins, or born of each other.

WILLIAM HAZLITT

Do more of what makes you happy...

Change it or accept it. The harsh truth of life
is that there will be times when we are unhappy.
Sometimes this will be caused by little things, at other times
it will be traumatic events which change the direction
of our lives. So what can you do when you are unhappy?
You have two choices – take action to remove the cause
of your unhappiness or, if this is not possible,
find ways of dealing with it that minimise the effects
and then accept your new reality.

MATHILDE & SÉBASTIEN FORESTIER

Do more of what makes you happy...

Everyone wants more, and yet, ironically,
the more we get the less we have.
We become so caught up in the process of
wanting we lose the joy of living. Having friendship
and love, sharing family time, these are
life's real treasures. As you make your plans
and set your goals, don't forget
to include happiness in the equation.

STUART & LINDA MACFARLANE

Do more of what makes you happy...

FEBRUARY 4

In the summer I sometimes sleep in a tree house in my garden and talk to the birds. I don't think I could live without a simple, basic contact with nature.

JOAN BAEZ

*Do more of what
makes you happy...*

NOVEMBER 28

Above all, let us never forget
that an act of goodness
is in itself an act of happiness.
It is the flower of a long inner life
of joy and contentment;
it tells of peaceful hours and days
on the sunniest heights of our soul.

COUNT MAURICE MAETERLINCK

Do more of what makes you happy...

Gather into yourself
like a bee,
the hours that fall open
under the bright shaft
of the sunripening in heat,
store them and
make of them honey days.

NUALA NI DHOMHNAILL

Do more of what makes you happy...

NOVEMBER 27

You must learn day by day,
year by year, to broaden your horizon.
The more things you love, the more
you are interested in,
the more you enjoy, the more
you are indignant about – the more
you have left when anything happens.

ETHEL BARRYMORE

Do more of what makes you happy...

FEBRUARY 6

The happiness you now have
is as beautiful and frail as a moth's wing.
Be gentle. Take care of it.

PAMELA DUGDALE

Do more of what makes you happy...

NOVEMBER 26

The cure for all the ills and wrongs,
the cares, the sorrows
and crimes of humanity, all lie
in that one word "love."
It is the divine vitality that
produces and restores life.
To each and every one of us it gives
the power of working miracles if we will.

LYDIA M. CHILD

Do more of what makes you happy...

FEBRUARY 7

You have
your brush,
you have
your colours,
you paint
paradise,
then in you go.

NIKOS KAZANTZAKIS

Do more of what makes you happy...

NOVEMBER 25

Loss leaves us empty —
but don't close your heart
and mind in grief.
Allow life to replenish you.
When sorrow comes
it seems impossible -
but new joys wait to fill the void.

PAM BROWN

Do more of what makes you happy...

FEBRUARY 8

It is one of the most beautiful compensations
of this life that no one can sincerely try
to help another without helping themself.

RALPH WALDO EMERSON

Do more of what makes you happy...

NOVEMBER 24

If you think that material comforts
are the only tickets to happiness,
you will not find what you are looking for.
Seek what fulfils your heart.
Don't let others "sell" you
objects of satisfaction. Find satisfaction
through your actions toward others.
The greatest reward is making a difference.

ERIN BROCKOVICH

Do more of what makes you happy...

FEBRUARY 9

We live in an Age of Frenzy.
Most people feel the need to check their phone
every two minutes and share photos with "Friends"
who are, in reality, just random strangers.
If this describes you it really is time for you to try meditation.
Meditation is all about training your
mind to focus purposely and achieving an
emotional calm and stable state.

LINDA GIBSON

Do more of what makes you happy...

If you feel no enthusiasm or inspiration on a particular day,
try to remember a joyful experience from your past.
The joy you got from your previous achievements
will carry you through. Very soon, you will not only reach,
but transcend your previous height. You are not fooling yourself;
you are only bringing happiness into your system,
and this happiness is confidence.

SRI CHINMOY

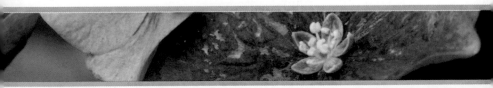

Do more of what makes you happy...

FEBRUARY 10

Precisely the least,
the softest, lightest,
a lizard's rustling,
a breath, a breeze,
a moment's glance —
it is little that makes
the best happiness.

FRIEDRICH WILHELM NIETZSCHE

Do more of what makes you happy...

NOVEMBER 22

Be yourself. Do not try to be someone that you are not. Be the person that makes you proud.

BRIAN CLYDE

Do more of what makes you happy...

FEBRUARY 11

To fill the hour
– that is happiness;
to fill the hour,
and leave no crevice
for a repentance
or an approval.

RALPH WALDO EMERSON

Do more of what makes you happy...

Happiness is being where you want to be –
with the person you want to be with –
doing the work you love.
Money has nothing to do with it.

PAM BROWN

Do more of what makes you happy...

FEBRUARY 12

You can, you know, just choose to be happy. Why not?
Keep telling yourself you are and you will be.
It's not really that hard to do. And, here's the thing,
if you choose to be happy it makes others happier
and so it goes around and around. On and on.

DALTON EXLEY

Do more of what makes you happy...

What is important, vitally important
for a happy life, is that you make the effort
to explore different hobbies and activities.
Taking the time to discover which ones provide
the magic for you. By doing so,
not only will you add considerably to your own
happiness but also to the happiness
of those around you.

MATHILDE FORESTIER

Do more of what makes you happy...

FEBRUARY 13

Here are the veins of your hand
and here are the veins of a leaf.
Here branches stretch out against the sky.
Here streams run to meet the river.
We are bound together. The same life
flows through all things.
Be happy in this unity, this continuity.

PAM BROWN

Do more of what makes you happy...

One of life's great secrets is surely to celebrate the small – the sight of a flower growing between the cracks in a pavement, the look on a young child's face when they're given a birthday present they've waited for long weeks to open.
Or something as simple as immersing ourselves in our favourite piece of music.

FROM "THE FRIENDSHIP BOOK OF FRANCIS GAY"

Do more of what makes you happy...

FEBRUARY 14

Doing what
you love
is freedom.
Loving what
you do
is happiness.

LANA DEL REY

Do more of what makes you happy...

Mindfulness helps you go home to the present.
And every time you go there and recognise
a condition of happiness that you have, happiness comes.

THICH NHAT HANH

Do more of what makes you happy...

So many people walk around
with a meaningless life. They seem half-asleep,
even when they're busy doing things they
think are important. This is because they're chasing
the wrong things. The way you get meaning
into your life is to devote yourself to loving others,
devote yourself to your community around you,
and devote yourself to creating something
that gives you purpose and meaning.

MORRIE SCHWARTZ

Do more of what makes you happy...

NOVEMBER 17

For centuries it has been known that dance has the power to help improve people's happiness. Plato said that "Of all the arts, dance is the one that most influences the soul". Modern research has shown that dance lowers anxiety, reduces stress and helps reduce depression. So what are you waiting for?

STUART & LINDA MACFARLANE

Do more of what makes you happy...

FEBRUARY 16

Happiness is
to complete a task well
and to one's
absolute satisfaction.

PAMELA DUGDALE

Do more of what makes you happy...

NOVEMBER 16

The secret of making something work in your life
is, first of all, the deep desire to make it work:
then the faith and belief that it can work:
then to hold that clear definite vision in your
consciousness and see it working out step by step,
without one thought of doubt or disbelief.

EILEEN CADDY

Do more of what makes you happy...

FEBRUARY 17

True happiness is of a retired nature, and an enemy
to pomp and noise; it arises, in the first place,
from the enjoyment of one's self, and, in the next, from
the friendship and conversation of a few select companions.
It loves shade and solitude, and naturally haunts groves
and fountains, fields and meadows; in short, it feels everything
it wants within itself, and receives no addition
from multitudes of witnesses and spectators.

JOSEPH ADDISON

Do more of what makes you happy...

NOVEMBER 15

HAPPINESS, IS LEARNING TO BE CONTENT WITH WHAT YOU DON'T HAVE.

KATHY LETTE

Do more of what makes you happy...

FEBRUARY 18

I suppose the moments one most enjoys are moments
– alone – when one unexpectedly stretches
something inside you that needs stretching.

GEORGIA O'KEEFE

Do more of what makes you happy...

NOVEMBER 14

There is great happiness in not wanting,
in not being something, in not going somewhere.

JIDDU KRISHNAMURTI

Do more of what makes you happy...

FEBRUARY 19

The secret of health for both mind and body
is not to mourn for the past, not to worry
about the future, or not to anticipate troubles,
but to live the present moment wisely and earnestly.

GAUTAMA BUDDHA

Do more of what makes you happy...

NOVEMBER 13

The only way to find happiness is to be true to yourself and to let all the rest of it – the money, the power, and the fame, should it one day come your way – be part of the result of your own individual, inner search for true identity and self-worth.

ERIN BROCKOVICH

Do more of what makes you happy...

FEBRUARY 20

The simplification of life
is one of the steps to inner peace.
A persistent simplification will create
an inner and outer well-being that
places harmony in one's life.
For me this began with the discovery
of the meaninglessness of
possessions beyond my actual
and immediate needs...

PEACE PILGRIM

Do more of what makes you happy...

Optimism is a happiness magnet.

MARY LOU RETTON

Do more of what makes you happy...

FEBRUARY 21

You are unique.
You are a beautiful
individual in a
beautiful world.
Celebrate your life.
Fill it with joy.

LINDA GIBSON

Do more of what makes you happy...

Happiness is when
what you think,
what you say, and what you do,
are in harmony.

MAHATMA GANDHI

Do more of what makes you happy...

FEBRUARY 22

Only lift your head and look about you.
People have found a glimpse
of happiness in dreadful places.
A shaft of spring sunshine on a prison wall.
A butterfly flitting above a city street.
The laughter of children in apparent desolation.
The touch of a dear familiar hand
in utter darkness.

PAM BROWN

Do more of what makes you happy...

FIND JOY IN LITTLE THINGS – AND THE GREAT THINGS WILL CREEP UP AND ASTONISH YOU.

PAM BROWN

Do more of what makes you happy...

The stresses and strains of today's hectic lifestyle puts us at risk of heart disease, stroke and many other diseases. Activities such as yoga, Pilates, meditation and exercising not only help us escape life's pressures but they have huge long term beneficial effects on our physical and mental health. Most of these can be done at home but joining a class will give you the additional opportunity to make new friends. Two fabulous reasons for giving them a try.

STUART & LINDA MACFARLANE

Do more of what makes you happy...

Being happy is not having some magical absence
of things to be unhappy about,
living some charmed existence. It's how,
in the end, you respond to any periods
of unhappiness in your own life. Many take their
whole life trying to get this balance right. But,
you can pretty much start right away. It's perfectly
possible for a change of attitude to be instant.

DALTON EXLEY

Do more of what makes you happy...

FEBRUARY 24

Nothing great was ever achieved
without enthusiasm. The way of life is wonderful;
it is by abandonment.

RALPH WALDO EMERSON

Do more of what makes you happy...

NOVEMBER 8

Fear less, hope more; eat less, chew more;
whine less, breathe more; talk less, say more; love more,
and all good things will be yours.

SWEDISH PROVERB

Do more of what makes you happy...

Being positive is
a happiness magnet.
Good things and good people
will be drawn to you.
Good things will happen to you,
and to all around you.

DALTON EXLEY

Do more of what makes you happy...

NOVEMBER 7

SOME DAYS THERE WON'T BE A SONG IN YOUR HEART. SING ANYWAY.

EMORY AUSTIN

Do more of what makes you happy...

FEBRUARY 26

Ten thousand flowers in spring,
the moon in autumn,
a cool breeze in summer,
snow in winter.
If your mind isn't clouded by
unnecessary things,
this is the best season of your life.

WU-MEN

Do more of what makes you happy...

NOVEMBER 6

When I have a problem or a worry, I go for
a long walk along a mountain trail. With each step that
I take a little bit of my worry falls by the wayside
and gets lost in the heather. By the time I get back home
the problem has shrunk to a manageable size.
I feel a great sense of inner satisfaction and elation.
There is no better therapy for stress than a peaceful walk –
it is quite literally the path to happiness.

LINDA GIBSON

Do more of what makes you happy...

Your thoughts
and your words
define your life.
Think positively and
affirm positive
words to enrich
your life positively.

LAILAH GIFTY AKITA

Do more of what makes you happy...

NOVEMBER 5

Read a poem. Read it again slowly.
Absorb the words. Caress the rhythm.
Peacefully enjoy.

BRIAN CLYDE

Do more of what makes you happy...

FEBRUARY 28 & 29

Surround yourself with
the beauty of nature
at every opportunity.
Let trees and flowers,
butterflies and bees
all add a smile to your life.

LINDA GIBSON

Do more of what makes you happy...

Whenever I run a city marathon there is sure to be
a child along the route who is attempting to hi-five all the runners.
Inevitably it's a happy, smiling child cheering on the runners
and shouting words of encouragement. I will always
hi-five the child back and exchange a smile.
What happens next is truly amazing; over the next mile
I feel much stronger and my body feels less painful.
And all because of a smile, a hi-five, and that wonderful
moment of happiness that I shared with an enthusiastic child.

STUART MACFARLANE

Do more of what makes you happy...

MARCH 1

BE AT
PEACE WITH
YOURSELF.

STUART & LINDA MACFARLANE

Do more of what makes you happy...

NOVEMBER 3

Never try to hunt down happiness.
It runs away and hides.
Be quiet of heart – and it will come to you.

PAMELA DUGDALE

Do more of what makes you happy...

As soon as possible after your special occasion,
find a peaceful place and go through the event in great detail.
This will help store your memories in the Good-Times section
of your mind. Regularly revisit these experiences
by dipping into your memory banks and reliving the delights.
This way the full wonder of your special moments
will be preserved forever.
Cherish your joyful memories – do not let them fade.

BRIAN CLYDE

Do more of what makes you happy...

There is beauty around us, in things large and small,
in friends, family, the countryside, a singing bird.
Stop to reflect, to give thanks, to contemplate the gift
of another day. Touch the wonders of life and rejoice.

ANTON CHEKHOV

Do more of what makes you happy...

Treasure does not usually come in ingots but in small coinage — a shining thunder cloud, a silver bird against a darkening sky, a frog, a flower, a thread of song.

PAM BROWN

Do more of what makes you happy...

NOVEMBER 1

How beautiful a day can be when kindness touches it!

GEORGE ELLISTON

Do more of what makes you happy...

MARCH 4

The more you praise and celebrate your life,
the more there is in life to celebrate.

OPRAH WINFREY

Do more of what makes you happy...

OCTOBER 31

Do not linger to gather flowers to keep them,
but walk on, for flowers will keep themselves
blooming all your way.

RABINDRANATH TAGORE

Do more of what makes you happy...

MARCH 5

I see happiness walking down the street. I hear happy people chatting and laughing. Wherever I go I see the joy of life. Yes, we all have many stresses and strains in our lives but happiness is our natural state. It is our penchant for happiness that lets us rise above all our worries and achieve all our dreams.

BRIAN CLYDE

Do more of what makes you happy...

OCTOBER 30

Your plan for work and happiness
should be big, imaginative and daring.
Strike out boldly for the things
you honestly want more
than anything else in the world.
The mistake is to put your sights too low,
not to raise them too high.

HENRY J. KAISER

Do more of what makes you happy...

MARCH 6

Happiness is the art of making a bouquet of those flowers within reach.

BOB GODDARD

Do more of what makes you happy...

Life's sweetest
things are the
quietest things...
a happy life consists
of tranquillity
of mind.

MARCUS TULLIUS CICERO

Do more of what makes you happy...

MARCH 7

Worrying interrupts happiness, leaks joy from today and robs the peace and promise of tomorrow.

DALTON EXLEY

Do more of what makes you happy...

OCTOBER 28

The fragrance always remains
in the hand
that gives the rose.

HEDA BEJAR

Do more of what makes you happy...

MARCH 8

The happiness of life is made up of
minute fractions – the little soon-forgotten
charities of a kiss, a smile, a kind look,
a heartfelt compliment in the disguise
of a playful raillery,
and the countless other infinitesimals
of pleasant thought and feeling.

SAMUEL TAYLOR COLERIDGE

Do more of what makes you happy...

OCTOBER 27

Why is it that it's a little annoying when someone tells you that you are as happy as you decide to be? Well, partly because you haven't embraced the idea that you could, one day, just decide to be happy. Deep down a part of you knows it's true. You could.

DALTON EXLEY

Do more of what makes you happy...

Find a peaceful mountain trail or path along
the side of a lake – somewhere that you really love
and enjoy. Go there often for walks.
Appreciate everything around you; the constantly
changing sky, the beautiful trees, the spectacular scenery.
Be part of nature, at one with the World.
Take its beauty and its peace. So that, during stressful
moments, you can be there again in spirit.

MATHILDE & SÉBASTIEN FORESTIER

Do more of what makes you happy...

OCTOBER 26

If you can come second in a race and feel as much joy
for the winner as you would have felt had you won,
then you have achieved the ultimate
level of self-confidence and inner strength.
BRIAN CLYDE

Do more of what makes you happy...

MARCH 10

Sometimes your joy
is the source of your smile,
but sometimes
your smile can be
the source of your joy.

THICH NHAT HANH

Do more of what makes you happy...

OCTOBER 25

Three grand essentials
to happiness in this life
are something to do,
something to love;
and something to hope for.

JOSEPH ADDISON

Do more of what makes you happy...

You have not lived a perfect day, even though you have earned your money, unless you have done something for someone who will never be able to repay you.

RUTH SMELTZER

Do more of what makes you happy...

OCTOBER 24

Whenever you are doing something
seemingly routine such as washing the dishes,
don't rush. Take your time. Notice every detail:
the sound of the water as it leaves the tap:
the feel of the bubbles on your hands:
the shapes it makes as it splashes onto the dishes:
the pattern on the plates and so on.
Appreciate everything, all these things are
important and have their own dignity.
Smile at this knowledge and be happy.

LINDA GIBSON

Do more of what makes you happy...

MARCH 12

There is a wonderful, mystical law of nature that the three things we crave most in life – happiness, freedom, and peace of mind – are always attained by giving them to someone else.

PEYTON CONWAY MARCH

Do more of what makes you happy...

Happiness does not come from
doing easy work but from the afterglow of satisfaction
that comes after the achievement of a difficult task
that demanded our best.

THEODORE I. RUBIN

Do more of what makes you happy...

MARCH 13

...cheerfulness keeps up
a kind of daylight in the mind,
and fills it with a steady
and perpetual serenity.

JOSEPH ADDISON

Do more of what makes you happy...

OCTOBER 22

It is not how much we have, but how much
we enjoy, that makes happiness.

CHARLES H. SPURGEON

Do more of what makes you happy...

MARCH 14

Avoid negative people.
Being with cheery,
optimistic people will help
lift your spirit
and encourage you
to see the positive side
of situations.

BRIAN CLYDE

Do more of what makes you happy...

OCTOBER 21

Of all happinesses, the most charming
is that of a firm and gentle friendship.
It sweetens all our cares, dispels our sorrows,
and counsels us in all extremities.

SENECA THE YOUNGER

Do more of what makes you happy...

MARCH 15

Flowers always make people better,
happier, and more helpful; they are sunshine,
food and medicine to the soul.

LUTHER BURBANK

Do more of what makes you happy...

OCTOBER 20

It is by believing,
hoping, loving,
and doing that
people find
joy and peace.

JOHN LANCASTER SPALDING

Do more of what makes you happy...

Planting trees
is deeply satisfying
and good for the soul,
especially on a winter's day.
It is the act of marking
a long time. What else
can a human do that
leans so far into the future?

MONTY DON

Do more of what makes you happy...

Picture yourself sitting on a rock beside
a stream. Ahead of you are stunning mountains
topped with glistening snow. To your left
are majestic oak trees that have stood proudly
for hundreds of years. Across the stream
a pair of deer are foraging for food.
Beautiful. Tranquil. Perfect. So why are you waiting?
Get out there and enjoy it now.

STUART MACFARLANE

Do more of what makes you happy...

MARCH 17

There is nothing we like to see so much as the gleam of pleasure in a person's eye when they feel that we have sympathised, understood, interested ourself in their welfare. These moments are the moments worth living.

DON MARQUIS

Do more of what makes you happy...

OCTOBER 18

They are happiest, be they royalty or peasant,
who find peace in their home.

JOHANN WOLFGANG VON GOETHE

Do more of what makes you happy...

MARCH 18

To walk in sunlight along
a lonely beach.
To sprawl in meadow grass.
To swim in the
transparency of water.
To come home
to those you love.
That's happiness.

PAM BROWN

Do more of what makes you happy...

OCTOBER 17

Let mystery have its place in you;
do not be always turning up
your whole soil with the ploughshare
of self-examination, but leave
a little fallow corner in your heart
ready for any seed the winds may bring,
and reserve a nook of shadow
for the passing bird.

HENRI FRÉDÉRIC AMIEL

Do more of what makes you happy...

MARCH 19

Half of the confusion
in the world comes
from not knowing
how little we need...
I live more simply now,
and with more peace.

RICHARD EVELYN BYRD

Do more of what makes you happy...

OCTOBER 16

When you are joyful, when you say yes to life and have fun and project positivity all around you, you become a sun in the centre of every constellation, and people want to be near you.

SHANNON L. ALDER

Do more of what makes you happy...

MARCH 20

If you want happiness for an hour, take a nap.
If you want happiness for a day, go fishing.
If you want happiness for a year, inherit a fortune.
If you want happiness for a lifetime, help someone.

CHINESE PROVERB

Do more of what makes you happy...

The only way we can keep what we have,
or feeling good about ourselves, is to give it away.

HAROLD BELMONT

Do more of what makes you happy...

Money, power – these are not the essential goals
for happiness. If anything, focusing on those will
keep you even further from the realisation
of your dreams. Money may buy you some temporary
degree of satisfaction, but it certainly doesn't bring
happiness… as for power, that is simply
lusting after control, most often out of a fear you really
don't have any – power or control.

ERIN BROCKOVICH

Do more of what makes you happy...

OCTOBER 14

I've learned that for a happy day, look for something bright and beautiful in nature. Listen for a beautiful sound, speak a kind word to some person, and do something nice for someone without their knowledge.

AUTHOR UNKNOWN

Do more of what makes you happy...

To be needed.
That is the vital thing.

PAM BROWN

Do more of what makes you happy...

OCTOBER 13

Is there any symbol more redolent of regeneration
than a seed, planted in rich compost, watered
and warmed, to produce a new shoot of green
in the spring? A tiny start, with the promise of plenty.
It has taken me a long time to learn
to look at those little leaves, and appreciate
their significance, but I understand it now.
And it has saved me from depression, even despair.

BARNEY BARDSLEY

Do more of what makes you happy...

MARCH 23

When you give and receive kindness
you are automatically richer than a millionaire.

NATASHA CLARKSON

Do more of what makes you happy...

OCTOBER 12

Do not give up on yourself.
Do not despair. Bad times pass.
It may be difficult to see
through the fog of despondency
but better times will follow.
Till then you must stay strong,
have faith in yourself.

MATHILDE & SÉBASTIEN FORESTIER

Do more of what makes you happy...

MARCH 24

Make each day your masterpiece.

JOHN WOODEN

Do more of what makes you happy...

OCTOBER 11

Happiness is having the courage to be better at something than you thought you could be.

PAM BROWN

Do more of what makes you happy...

MARCH 25

Happiness is being aware of what is going on in the present moment, free from both clinging and aversion. A happy person cherishes the wonders taking place in the present moment — a cool breeze, the morning sky, a golden flower, a violet bamboo tree, the smile of a child. A happy person can appreciate these things without being bound by them.

THICH NHAT HANH

Do more of what makes you happy...

OCTOBER 10

Share your worries.
Talk them through
with someone you trust.
Talking will help put them
in perspective and help you
free yourself from
needless stress.

STUART & LINDA MACFARLANE

Do more of what makes you happy...

Be gentle, patient, humble and courteous to all, but
especially be gentle and patient with yourself.
I think that many of your troubles arise from an exaggerated
anxiety, a secret impatience with your own faults.

PERE HYACINTHE BESSON

Do more of what makes you happy...

OCTOBER 9

It is not doing
the thing
we like to do,
but liking the thing
we have to do,
that makes life blessed.

JOHANN WOLFGANG VON GOETHE

Do more of what makes you happy...

Happiness itself is sufficient excuse.
Wise people have an inward sense of what is beautiful,
and the highest wisdom is
to trust this intuition and be guided by it.

ARISTOTLE

Do more of what makes you happy...

OCTOBER 8

I have found that the happiest people are
those who do the most for others;
the most miserable are those who do the least.

BOOKER T. WASHINGTON

Do more of what makes you happy...

MARCH 28

Money can't buy you happiness.
But debt can buy you great unhappiness.
That is a very, very sad fact of life.
As far as reasonably possible, avoid getting into debt.
Do not buy anything unless it is absolutely necessary
and you have the money to pay for it.
Borrowed money is inevitably expensive but perhaps
a greater expense is the worry and stress
the debt is likely to cause you.

BRIAN CLYDE

Do more of what makes you happy...

Most ordinary things — but seen
with a new perception. Hedges laced with
spangled spider webs. A dazzle of new leaves.
A splendid cat sprawled tiger-like along a wall.
A flurry of snow. Gifts of every season, of every
time of day. And given only to those
prepared to see. People like you.

PAMELA DUGDALE

Do more of what makes you happy...

MARCH 29

ALL SORROW AND ALL JOY COME FROM LOVE.

MEISTER ECKHART

Do more of what makes you happy...

OCTOBER 6

If you want to be happy, be.
Stop a moment, cease your work,
look around you.

LEO TOLSTOY

Do more of what makes you happy...

MARCH 30

Gratefulness is the key to a happy life that we hold in our hands, because if we are not grateful, then no matter how much we have we will not be happy – because we will always want to have something else or something more.

DAVID STEINDL-RAST

Do more of what makes you happy...

OCTOBER 5

People spend a lifetime searching for happiness;
looking for peace. They chase idle dreams,
addictions, religions, even other people, hoping to fill
the emptiness that plagues them. The irony is
the only place they ever needed to search was within.

RAMONA L. ANDERSON

Do more of what makes you happy...

MARCH 31

The capacity to care is the thing which gives life its deepest meaning and significance.

PABLO CASALS

Do more of what makes you happy...

H appiness is a perfume you cannot pour on others without getting a few drops on yourself.

RALPH WALDO EMERSON

Do more of what makes you happy...

APRIL 1

You can't help someone uphill
without getting closer to the top yourself.

PROVERB

Do more of what makes you happy...

OCTOBER 3

Believe in yourself. Trust in your feelings.
Trust in your ideas. Plan your happiness.
Make time for purposeful contemplation then
take action for success and happiness.

BRIAN CLYDE

Do more of what makes you happy...

APRIL 2

Is life moving too fast? Take a few minutes to try
this simple meditation exercise:
– Sit or lie in a comfortable position.
– Close your eyes.
– Shut out all distractions and focus purely on your breathing.
– Feel the air slowly going in and out of your lungs.
– If your mind wanders, return your focus back
to your breathing. Initially do this exercise for two minutes.
If you find it beneficial increase it for a longer period.

STUART & LINDA MACFARLANE

Do more of what makes you happy...

OCTOBER 2

The Ancient Greeks told us that someone
that finds discontentment in one place
is not likely to find happiness in another.
It's as old as time. Happiness isn't something we can
get from owning something. Or moving somewhere.
Happiness is how we see life. How it fills us.
Is beyond us. How it passes through our children,
into new lives. Into everything. This is happiness.

DALTON EXLEY

Do more of what makes you happy...

APRIL 3

I have found such joy
in things that fill my quiet days –
a curtain's blowing grace,
A growing plant upon a window sill,
A rose fresh-cut and placed within a vase,
A table cleared, a lamp beside a chair,
And books I long have loved
beside me there.

GRACE NOLL CROWELL

Do more of what makes you happy...

DO YOU WANT TO BE HAPPY? THEN MAKE YOUR LIFE SOULFULLY SIMPLE.

SRI CHINMOY

Do more of what makes you happy...

APRIL 4

Nothing really matters except
what you do now
in this instant of time.

EILEEN CADDY

Do more of what makes you happy...

SEPTEMBER 30

WHEN THE
STRIVING CEASES,
THERE IS
LIFE WAITING
AS A GIFT.

SAUL BELLOW

Do more of what makes you happy...

When you see a need, ask yourself if you can help to fill it. Give yourself to life. Give yourself to love. Love is your secret talisman. The more you give, the more you have to give, and the more you receive. As you help, you are helped. And as you heal others, you yourself are healed.

SUSAN L. TAYLOR

Do more of what makes you happy...

SEPTEMBER 29

In the tough moments, and every life
has them, take a step back! Stop!
Cherish the moment you are in —
feel the air as you take a soft breath in.
Hear the air as you slowly exhale.
Feel your chest gently rise and fall.
Now peacefully move ahead.

BRIAN CLYDE

Do more of what makes you happy...

APRIL 6

Flowers and birds
you've never seen.
Friends as yet have never met.
Be brave. Be curious.
Be courteous.
Discover a wider world.

PAMELA DUGDALE

Do more of what makes you happy...

SEPTEMBER 28

Don't be too busy, too serious, too sensible –
at least, not all the time! Remember to have a little fun,
enjoy a little nonsense, a sprinkling of dreams,
even a few daydreams, to balance life's doing.
Make the most, too, of life's small joys and pleasures
as well as its great happinesses. It will help you to cope
all the better with the ups and down of life!

FROM "THE FRIENDSHIP BOOK OF FRANCIS GAY"

Do more of what makes you happy...

APRIL 7

Nothing of value can be done without joy.
Cultivate happiness in yourself and in others, and you will wonder
at the beauty, the richness, the power that come to you.

HELEN KELLER (BORN BOTH DEAF AND BLIND)

Do more of what makes you happy...

SEPTEMBER 27

Did you know that even just thirty minutes of exercise five times a week will make you healthier and happier? Of course you did. So why aren't you doing it?

MATHILDE & SÉBASTIEN FORESTIER

Do more of what makes you happy...

We search for happiness everywhere, but we are like Tolstoy's fabled beggar who spent his life sitting on a pot of gold, begging for pennies from every passer-by, unaware that his fortune was right under him the whole time. Your treasure – your perfection – is within you already. But to claim it, you must leave the busy commotion of the mind and abandon the desires of the ego and enter into the silence of the heart.

ELIZABETH GILBERT

Do more of what makes you happy...

SEPTEMBER 26

Sixty seconds in every minute – 3,600 in every hour – each one a precious diamond to cherish and enjoy.

STUART & LINDA MACFARLANE

Do more of what makes you happy...

Cherish your friends. Keep an interest in them.
Keep them close. Friends and family
are the pillars upon which our happiness is built.

LINDA GIBSON

Do more of what makes you happy...

SEPTEMBER 25

Fill each day. Give it your youth, your health, your abilities, your hope – so that your whole life will be a wonder. And your memories sweet.

PAMELA DUGDALE

Do more of what makes you happy...

APRIL 10

Stop what you are doing.
Stop what you are doing
right now. Take one minute,
this minute, for yourself.
Find a happy thought
and let it be everything.
Let it fill your imagination for one
beautiful minute.

STUART & LINDA MACFARLANE

Do more of what makes you happy...

SEPTEMBER 24

Often people attempt to live their
lives backwards: they try to have more things,
or more money, in order to do more of what they
want so they will be happier. The way it
actually works is the reverse. You must first be
who you really are, then do what you need to do,
in order to have what you want.

MARGARET YOUNG

Do more of what makes you happy...

APRIL 11

Don't be
a complainer,
a moaner
or a pessimist.
That's the opposite
of becoming
happy.

DALTON EXLEY

Do more of what makes you happy...

Practice hope on
little things —
the first snowdrop,
the first swallow,
first smile, first word,
first step.

CHARLOTTE GRAY

Do more of what makes you happy...

Happiness is having a sense of self
– not a feeling of being perfect but of being good enough
and knowing that you are in the process of growth,
of being, of achieving levels of joy.

LEO BUSCAGLIA

Do more of what makes you happy...

SEPTEMBER 22

One is happy as a result of
one's own efforts, once one knows the
necessary ingredients of happiness –
simple tastes, a certain degree of courage,
self-denial to a point, love of work,
and above all, a clear conscience.
Happiness is no vague dream, of that
I now feel certain.

GEORGE SAND (AMANDINE-LUCILE-AURORE DUPIN)

Do more of what makes you happy...

Those who have little
have more room in their lives for joy.

PAM BROWN

Do more of what makes you happy...

SEPTEMBER 21

One of the most tragic things I know about human nature is that all of us tend to put off living. We are all dreaming of some magical rose garden over the horizon – instead of enjoying the roses that are blooming outside our windows today.

DALE CARNEGIE

Do more of what makes you happy...

APRIL 14

Love the moment. Flowers grow out of dark moments.
Therefore, each moment is vital.
It affects the whole. Life is a succession of such moments
and to live each, is to succeed.

CORITA KENT

Do more of what makes you happy...

SEPTEMBER 20

Take time to appreciate the beauty and wonder
of the changing seasons. Even if just for a few minutes each
day sit in the same spot by a window. Observe the frost
and snow of winter covering the landscape, the
first flowers pushing through harsh earth, fledgling birds
chirping at their parents for food. We live in a beautiful world.
It is a privilege to be part of it. Do not miss it.

LINDA GIBSON

Do more of what makes you happy...

APRIL 15

To any sensitive person who reads the paper,
every morning can be a hard blow;
murders, suicides, air crashes, war, violence, disease,
poverty – in every country on the face of the earth.
If you are sensitive, your heart will melt in grief.
Yet the greatest joy lies in devoting
your life to the amelioration of this sorrow.
The greatest fulfilment comes to you when you
dedicate your life to bring some of these tragedies
to an end, to wipe the tears away
from the eyes of a few people.

EKNATH EASWARAN

Do more of what makes you happy...

SEPTEMBER 19

Happiness is
scattered through our
lives like daisies
through a meadow.
We have only to look
and touch to discover it.

PAM BROWN

Do more of what makes you happy...

Many people wake up on Monday mornings with dread.
They reluctantly drag themselves off to do jobs that give them
no pleasure. On the positive side they have
nice homes, fancy cars and the latest hi-tech equipment...
but not the time to appreciate it all.
Suppose that, by taking a cut in income, you could swap
this for a job that you really love – one that you could do
with pride and which brought you great pleasure?
It is well worth considering, give it thought.

BRIAN CLYDE

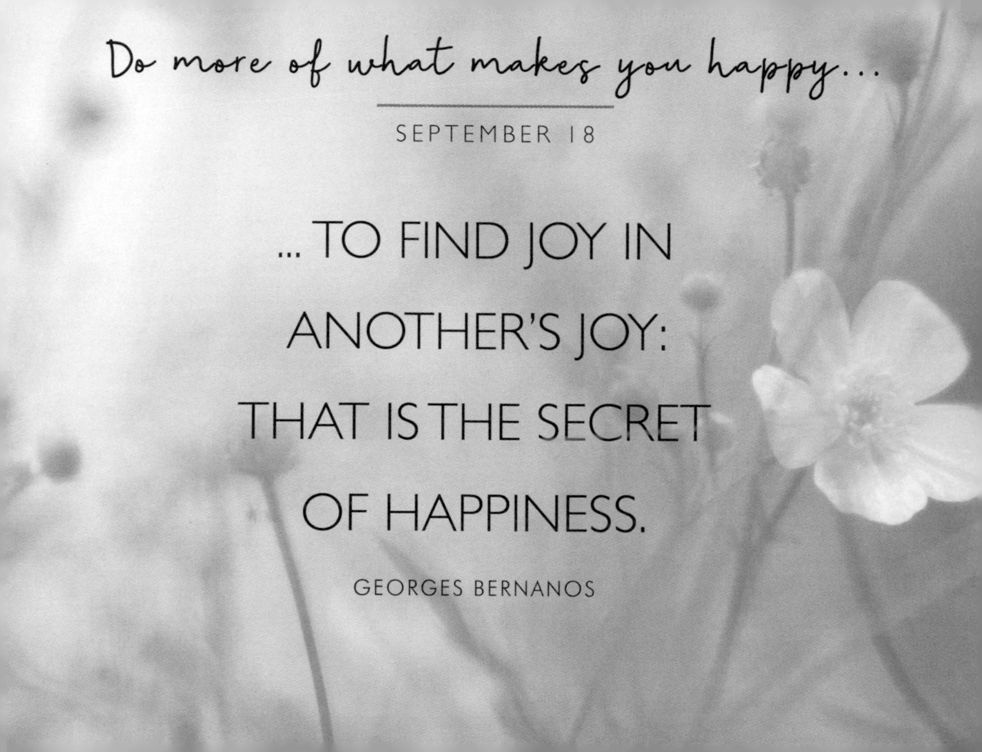

Do more of what makes you happy...

... TO FIND JOY IN
ANOTHER'S JOY:
THAT IS THE SECRET
OF HAPPINESS.

GEORGES BERNANOS

Do more of what makes you happy...

APRIL 17

It's just the little
homely things,
The unobtrusive,
friendly things,
The "Won't-you-let-
me-help-you" things...
that make the world
seem bright.

AUTHOR UNKNOWN

Do more of what makes you happy...

SEPTEMBER 17

Actively look for new challenges.
Whether it be completing a park run, knitting a jumper or
parachuting from an aeroplane, always have
something new and interesting to try. Fill your horizon
with excitement and adventure.

STUART & LINDA MACFARLANE

Do more of what makes you happy...

Find ways to be calm; meditation, yoga
or simply reading a book. Develop techniques that allow you
to escape from the stresses and strains of life.

LINDA GIBSON

Do more of what makes you happy...

SEPTEMBER 16

A man asked Lord Buddha
"I want Happiness"
Lord Buddha said
"First remove 'I' that's ego.
Then remove 'want' that's desire.
See now you are
left with only 'Happiness'".

AUTHOR UNKNOWN

Do more of what makes you happy...

APRIL 19

Take time to be friendly –
It is the road to happiness.
Take time to dream –
It is hitching your wagon to a star.
Take time to love and to be loved –
It is the privilege of the gods.
Take time to look around –
It is too short a day to be selfish.
Take time to laugh –
It is the music of the soul.

FROM AN OLD ENGLISH SAMPLER

Do more of what makes you happy...

For the past eighty years I have started each day in the same manner. It is not a mechanical routine but something essential to my daily life. I go to the piano, and I play two preludes and fugues of Bach. I cannot think of doing otherwise. It is a sort of benediction on the house. But that is not its only meaning for me. It is a rediscovery of the world of which I have the joy of being a part. It fills me with awareness of the wonder of life, with a feeling of the incredible marvel of being a human being.

PABLO CASALS

Do more of what makes you happy...

APRIL 20

Appreciate the moment. It is precious,
never to be repeated.
But if you experience it fully
you can revisit it as often as you wish.

BRIAN CLYDE

Do more of what makes you happy...

SEPTEMBER 14

When you realise you are
already complete, you've started,
you're on the way.
Acceptance, of everything, helps.
That doesn't mean you won't still want
to change many things, but it's against
a backdrop of acceptance
and not as a burden constantly
weighing you down.

DALTON EXLEY

Do more of what makes you happy...

APRIL 21

Service to a just cause rewards the worker with more real happiness and satisfaction than any other venture of life.

CARRIE CHAPMAN CATT

Do more of what makes you happy...

SEPTEMBER 13

Chase happiness and it will evade you.
Go about your work to the very best of your ability –
and find that happiness settles on your shoulder.

ODILE DORMEUIL

Do more of what makes you happy...

APRIL 22

The first step toward peace of mind is
to sincerely feel that we are not indispensable.
We lack peace of mind because
we feel that others need something from us,
or we need something from others.
But the moment we can sincerely feel
that we are not indispensable,
we will not have to go anywhere to get peace,
for peace will immediately come to us.

SRI CHINMOY

Do more of what makes you happy...

SEPTEMBER 12

Some of the most common ideas for spreading
happiness are simple things like smiling,
saying thank you, giving time or listening to another person
and always being positive. Try to make these
habits of a lifetime. But imagine if you developed
the one simple habit of smiling at people –
for the rest of your life. That alone would mean
that you spread happiness wherever you go.

HELEN EXLEY

Do more of what makes you happy...

APRIL 23

Grow your own laughter. Catch your own dreams.
Fashion each day of your life
with excitement, joy and contentment.

AMANDA BELL

Do more of what makes you happy...

The art of living lies less in eliminating our troubles than in growing with them.

BERNARD M. BARUCH

Do more of what makes you happy...

APRIL 24

I struggle to live for the beauty of a pansy,
for a little black baby's song,
for my lover's laugh.
I struggle for the blaze of pink
across the evening sky...
I struggle for life and the pursuit of its happiness.
I struggle to fill my house with joy.

STEPHANIE BYRD

Do more of what makes you happy...

SEPTEMBER 10

Thankfulness transforms the world.
Turns acquaintances into friends.
Makes mediocre days feel good.
Helps dry tears of sorrow.
Opens eyes to the wonders of nature.
When we appreciate our
blessings everything becomes
much more pleasurable.

MATHILDE FORESTIER

Do more of what makes you happy...

APRIL 25

Live in each season
as it passes,
breathe the air,
drink the drink,
taste the fruit,
and resign yourself
to the influences of each.

HENRY DAVID THOREAU

Do more of what makes you happy...

Happiness is found in our achievements.
For some this is running a marathon race
to raise money or it's climbing Everest.
Whatever the challenge there is great
satisfaction in pushing ourselves just a little bit
further than we thought possible.

MATHILDE & SÉBASTIEN FORESTIER

Do more of what makes you happy...

APRIL 26

To become incredibly skilful at something,
however small, can be one of the greatest happinesses.

PAM BROWN

Do more of what makes you happy...

SEPTEMBER 8

YOU HAVE TO SNIFF OUT JOY, KEEP YOUR NOSE TO THE JOY-TRAIL.

BUFFY SAINTE-MARIE

Do more of what makes you happy...

APRIL 27

You will find
as you look back upon
your life that the moments
when you have really lived
are the moments
when you have done things
in the spirit of love.

HENRY DRUMMOND

Do more of what makes you happy...

Happy is harder than money.
Anyone who thinks money will make them happy,
doesn't have money.

DAVID GEFFEN

Do more of what makes you happy...

APRIL 28

Inner contentment is achieved by being
grateful for what you have rather than
being on a never ending
spiral of trying to get better things,
become famous or have lots of power.
If you are content with little then
you have everything that you will ever need.

MATHILDE FORESTIER

Do more of what makes you happy...

SEPTEMBER 6

Numerous studies have shown that dancing improves happiness and increases self-esteem. It would seem that participants in dances where precision of movement is less important, such as ceilidhs and country dance are likely to laugh a lot and have great fun. But, if you don't like the idea of going to formal dance classes, dancing at home is just as beneficial. There are even Apps that allow you to dance along to people from all around the world. So get dancing. Get laughing. Get happy.

STUART & LINDA MACFARLANE

Do more of what makes you happy...

APRIL 29

The beauty of the trees,
the softness of the air, the fragrance
of the grass, speak to me...
the faintness of the stars,
the freshness of the morning,
the dewdrop on the flower, speak to me...
and my heart soars.

CHIEF DAN GEORGE, COAST SALISH

Do more of what makes you happy...

SEPTEMBER 5

Happiness depends on what you can give. Not what you can get.

MAHATMA GANDHI

Do more of what makes you happy...

APRIL 30

Those who bring sunshine to the lives of others cannot keep it from themselves.

SIR JAMES M. BARRIE

Do more of what makes you happy...

SEPTEMBER 4

Don't evaluate your life in terms of achievements,
trivial or monumental, along the way... instead, wake up
and appreciate everything you encounter along the path.
Enjoy the flowers that are there for your pleasure.
Tune in to the sunrise, the little children, the laughter,
the rain, and the birds. Drink it all in...
there is no way to happiness; happiness is the way.

DR. WAYNE W. DYER

Do more of what makes you happy...

Carpenters
bend wood;
fletchers
bend arrows;
wise people
fashion themselves.

GAUTAMA BUDDHA

Do more of what makes you happy...

SEPTEMBER 3

The man who preserves his selfhood ever calm and unshaken by the storms of existence — not a leaf as it were, astir on the trees; not a ripple upon the surface of a shining pool — his, in the mind of the unlettered sage, is the ideal attitude and conduct of life.

DR. CHARLES ALEXANDER EASTMAN

Do more of what makes you happy...

Find time for silence and solitude.
Constant noise, constant activity, constant distractions
are a burden. They restrict your enjoyment of the present
and your ability to visualise and plan your future.

MATHILDE & SÉBASTIEN FORESTIER

Do more of what makes you happy...

...the effect of seeing a child's smile compared
to the same stimulation which would be had from eating
2,000 chocolate bars or receiving £16,000 in cash.

RESEARCH BY HEWLETT PACKARD

Do more of what makes you happy...

MAY 3

When we see someone suffering, if we touch her
with compassion, she will receive our comfort and love,
and we will also receive comfort and love.

THICH NHAT HANH

Do more of what makes you happy...

SEPTEMBER 1

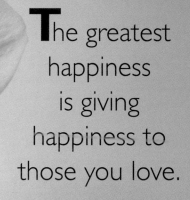

The greatest happiness is giving happiness to those you love.

PAMELA DUGDALE

Do more of what makes you happy...

MAY 4

Surprisingly, for many who dream
winning the lottery
is the answer to all their problems,
long term happiness
is really found through being needed
and by helping others.

DALTON EXLEY

Do more of what makes you happy...

AUGUST 31

It is easy in the world to live after the world's opinion; it is easy in solitude to live after our own; but the great person is the one who in the midst of the crowd keeps with perfect sweetness the independence of solitude.

RALPH WALDO EMERSON

Do more of what makes you happy...

MAY 5

Be nice to people.
Make the effort to say thoughtful things
and do little acts of kindness whenever possible.
It does not have to be a huge gesture
— simply holding a door open for someone
or saying, "Have a nice day"
will not only make them feel happier
but will make you feel happier too.

BRIAN CLYDE

Do more of what makes you happy...

AUGUST 30

The most complete happiness
is to work at something
you love, and to do it to the best
of your ability.

ODILE DORMEUIL

Do more of what makes you happy...

MAY 6

Each morning give yourself a gift.
A smile. Wear it all day. Be proud to be happy.
Be proud to be you.

LINDA GIBSON

Do more of what makes you happy...

Contentment, and indeed usefulness,
comes as the infallible result of great acceptances,
great humilities — of not trying
to make ourselves this or that to conform
to some dramatized version of ourselves,
but of surrendering ourselves to the fullness of life —
of letting life flow through us.

DAVID GRAYSON

Do more of what makes you happy...

MAY 7

The secret of success,
of happiness,
is to value every moment of each day.

PAM BROWN

Do more of what makes you happy...

There is a feature on your phone
which will help you find
tranquillity and calm.
It is called the "Off Button".

BRIAN CLYDE

Do more of what makes you happy...

MAY 8

Adopt a special tree — make it your friend.
My best tree friend is a beautiful Lime Tree on the banks
of the River Ness close to the finish of the Loch Ness Marathon.
Each year for the past fourteen years I have taken a moment
to stop at it and connect with it by putting my hands against
its bark. It is a precious tree to me. I feel as if it has been
part of my running journey over the years. I feel as if it
watches over me as I finish the race. It gives me great joy.
Find your own special trees and make new friends.

STUART MACFARLANE

Do more of what makes you happy...

AUGUST 27

Wealth, fame, and talent alone are not enough to make us happy. When they occur independently of genuine values, they only throw into greater relief the true poverty and slavery of our lives.

THE MONKS OF NEW SKETE

Do more of what makes you happy...

All our dreams can come true
– if we have the courage to pursue them.

WALT DISNEY

Do more of what makes you happy...

AUGUST 26

There is only one world, the world pressing against you
at this minute. There is only one minute
in which you are alive, this one. Happiness
is not a goal dependent on some future event,
it could be with us all the time if we only made
the effort to recognise it. And surely
the best way to live is by accepting each minute
as an unrepeatable miracle. Which is exactly what it is.

ROY BOLITHO

Do more of what makes you happy...

MAY 10

I slept and I dreamed that life is all joy.
I woke and I saw that life is all service. I served
and I saw that service is joy.

KAHLIL GIBRAN

Do more of what makes you happy...

AUGUST 25

I have found that there is a
tremendous joy in giving.
It is a very important part of the joy of living.

WILLIAM BLACK

Do more of what makes you happy...

MAY 11

Find something
that you love to do.
Set aside time for it.
However drab the everyday
– those moments
will light up your life,
give it purpose
and transform it.

PAMELA DUGDALE

Do more of what makes you happy...

AUGUST 24

Be at peace as you work.
If you can do that then your
work will be done well,
Your thoughts, values you hold,
will be in the work and will
permeate the whole process.
It will be good.

HELEN EXLEY

Do more of what makes you happy...

MAY 12

You know, when I am troubled
I will look to the hills. Whether snow-capped
or patterned with summer clouds, their age-old,
cool detachment from the hurly-burly of daily life
will calm the mind. They will give
a new perspective to concerns and worries.

AUTHOR UNKNOWN

Do more of what makes you happy...

AUGUST 23

Yesterday's gone. Tomorrow's invented.
We only ever have today, this moment. This life.
Don't waste it. At least stop to enjoy it.
So brief a spell we have, and if happiness, like some magic dust,
touches us, even briefly, then smile and treasure it.

DALTON EXLEY

Do more of what makes you happy...

MAY 13

I have found joy in simple things:
a plain, clean room,
a nut-brown loaf of bread,
a cup of milk, a kettle as it sings,
the shelter of a roof above my head,
and in a leaf-laced square along the floor,
where yellow sunlight
glimmers through a door.

GRACE NOLL CROWELL

Do more of what makes you happy...

AUGUST 22

Remember the happiness of being
a young child: nursery rhymes, teddy bears, hugs.
Remember how you felt safe and loved.
Everything was so much simpler then. So perfect.
Sadly, as we become adults, we complicate things
and often lose the joy of living.
Simplify your life; read books, sing songs,
dance and have lots and lots and lots of hugs.

STUART & LINDA MACFARLANE

Do more of what makes you happy...

Reflect upon your blessings, of which
every man had plenty, not on your past misfortunes,
of which all men have some.

CHARLES DICKENS

Do more of what makes you happy...

Look for little pleasures, and the small, beautiful things in life. Do not let them escape your notice. They are bright, golden threads in the cloth of life.

FROM "THE FRIENDSHIP BOOK OF FRANCIS GAY"

Do more of what makes you happy...

MAY 15

Have fun! Enjoy the years that lie ahead.
Open your arms to all delight
— of flowers and music, every lovely thing.
Of bold adventure and astonishment. Of love.
Of friends you've yet to meet.
Be brave. Be curious. Be courteous.
Discover a wider world.

MARGOT THOMSON

Do more of what makes you happy...

AUGUST 20

Think of times when you were happiest. It is very likely that these will be times involving family or friends. For happiness is all about love and friendship. It is about sharing time, sharing thoughts, sharing experiences and sharing love.

BRIAN CLYDE

Do more of what makes you happy...

MAY 16

Every word and every being
come knocking at your door, bringing you their mystery.
If you are open to them,
they will flood you with their riches.

IRÉNÉE GUILANE DIOH

Do more of what makes you happy...

AUGUST 19

ONE SHOULD NOT SEEK HAPPINESS, BUT HAPPY PEOPLE.

COCO CHANEL

Do more of what makes you happy...

MAY 17

Be sincere in
your thoughts,
Be pure in your feelings.
You will not have to run
after happiness.
Happiness will run
after you.

SRI CHINMOY

Do more of what makes you happy...

AUGUST 18

Don't rely on someone else for your happiness and self-worth. Only you can be responsible for that. If you can't love and respect yourself – no one else will be able to make that happen. Accept who you are – completely; the good and the bad – and make changes as YOU see fit – not because you think someone else wants you to be different.

STACY CHARTER

Do more of what makes you happy...

MAY 18

Avoid anything in excess.
Avoid anything that may damage your health.
If something controls you
rather than you controlling it
then you are at grave risk. Take steps to change.
Take steps to get back in control.
If necessary get help and advice.
Only when you are free will you find
peace and happiness.

STUART & LINDA MACFARLANE

Do more of what makes you happy...

AUGUST 17

Happiness is not a goal;
it is a by-product of a life well lived.

ELEANOR ROOSEVELT

Do more of what makes you happy...

MAY 19

Life is a journey,
and if you fall in love with the journey,
you will be in love forever.

PETER HAGERTY

Do more of what makes you happy...

AUGUST 16

Take a day off from all negative thoughts.
Banish them. If they try to creep back in, think of
something nice as a distraction. Do not give those nasty thoughts
a chance. After a successful day like this you will feel
much more energised... now do the same for a whole month.

LINDA MACFARLANE

Do more of what makes you happy...

MAY 20

Be willing to say "No".
Be your own person.
Make your own choices.
Be resolute and strong.
Be amazing.

BRIAN CLYDE

Do more of what makes you happy...

AUGUST 15

To be without some of the things you want
is an indispensable part of happiness. Live your own.

BERTRAND RUSSELL

Do more of what makes you happy...

MAY 21

Hope is itself a species of happiness,
and, perhaps the chief happiness
which this world affords...

DR. SAMUEL JOHNSON

Do more of what makes you happy...

AUGUST 14

The way to choose happiness
is to follow what is right
and real and the truth for you.
You can never be happy
living someone else's dream.
Live your own.

OPRAH WINFREY

Do more of what makes you happy...

MAY 22

When life gives a hundred reasons to break down
and cry, show life that you have
a thousand reasons to smile and laugh. Stay strong.

AUTHOR UNKNOWN

Do more of what makes you happy...

AUGUST 13

It's often possible to turn negative situations into positive. Never feel a situation is all negative. There's a counterpart that is positive. Look for it, reach for it, utilize it — it will offset the negative.

BEAR HEART (MUSKOGEE)

Do more of what makes you happy...

Part of the happiness of life consists
not in fighting battles but avoiding them.
A masterly retreat is in itself a victory.

NORMAN VINCENT PEALE

Do more of what makes you happy...

AUGUST 12

Let happiness be yours today as you find what brings you beauty... the fresh flowers on your table, the fragile seashell on your desk.

SUSAN SQUELLATI FLORENCE

Do more of what makes you happy...

MAY 24

Some people
are foolish enough to imagine
that wealth and power and fame
satisfy our hearts:
but they never do, unless
they are used to create and distribute
happiness in the world.

HELEN KELLER (BORN BOTH DEAF AND BLIND)

Do more of what makes you happy...

It is easy to become worried and even
depressed with everything that's going on in the World
right now. Global warming, super viruses
and political unrest. Sometimes you need to switch off
from it all and take stock of your own life.
Focus on the positive and do not allow yourself
to be overwhelmed by things that you cannot control.

LINDA GIBSON

Do more of what makes you happy...

MAY 25

Search for a job that gives you satisfaction.
Search for chances.
Search out beauty and discovery.
Happiness comes as part of the package.

PAMELA DUGDALE

Do more of what makes you happy...

Happiness does not come boxed and labelled.
Cannot be supplied by manufacturers.
Grows wild. Is all about you. Free.

HANNAH C. KLEIN

Do more of what makes you happy...

Happiness is built on simple foundations
– the love of beauty, a sense of humour,
the gift of good friends.

FROM "THE FRIENDSHIP BOOK OF FRANCIS GAY"

Do more of what makes you happy...

AUGUST 9

The crowning fortune is to be born to some pursuit which finds you employment and happiness, whether it be to make baskets or broadswords, or canals, or statues, or songs.

RALPH WALDO EMERSON

Do more of what makes you happy...

MAY 27

Those whose minds are shaped by selfless thoughts
give joy when they speak or act.
Joy follows them like a shadow that never leaves them.

GAUTAMA BUDDHA

Do more of what makes you happy...

AUGUST 8

...forget pursuing happiness. Pin your hopes
on work, on family, on learning, on knowing, on loving.
Forget pursuing happiness;
pursue these other things and happiness will come.

WILLIAM J. BENNETT

Do more of what makes you happy...

Some people seek happiness all their lives
and only find silver and gold.
Only when it is too late
do they realise that very often wealth
is accumulated at the expense of happiness.
For the harder you try and the longer you spend
piling coin upon coin, the less time you will have
for the things that really matter.
Happiness is the only commodity
in which it is worth investing.

MATHILDE FORESTIER

Do more of what makes you happy...

AUGUST 7

Why not seize
the pleasure at once?
How often is happiness
destroyed by preparation,
foolish preparation!

JANE AUSTEN

Do more of what makes you happy...

Always laugh when you can;
It is cheap medicine.

LORD BYRON

Do more of what makes you happy...

AUGUST 6

To have lived long enough to see the sun,
the dapple of leaves, star-studded skies and kindly faces –
to have heard the wind, birdsong, loving voices,
to have touched a little cat, a woollen blanket,
a flower, to have tasted clear water, fresh bread, honey,
to have breathed the perfume of a rose –
is enough to make any life worth the living.

CHARLOTTE GRAY

Do more of what makes you happy...

When the fog of hopelessness is thickest
you must journey with the greatest care.
Go slowly. No hasty decisions. No sudden turns.
For now you are in survival mode,
moving forward step by step. But this fog will clear.
Slowly it will disperse. And you will emerge
into the sunshine a survivor.
Stronger and wiser for your experience.

LINDA GIBSON

Do more of what makes you happy...

HAPPINESS IS FOUND IN SERVICE – NEVER IN DOMINANCE.

PAMELA DUGDALE

Do more of what makes you happy...

MAY 31

Life is not made up
of great sacrifices and duties,
but of little things;
in which smiles and kindness
given habitually
are what win
and preserve the heart.

SIR HUMPHREY DAVY

Do more of what makes you happy...

AUGUST 4

There is no better way of helping yourself
than by helping others. Whether it is sharing your skills
or helping at a homeless shelter, you
will be rewarded with a huge sense of satisfaction.
There is a tremendous joy that comes from
being able to provide comfort to those in need.

BRIAN CLYDE

Do more of what makes you happy...

There is only one way to happiness
and that is to cease worrying about things which
are beyond the power of our will.

EPICTETUS

Do more of what makes you happy...

AUGUST 3

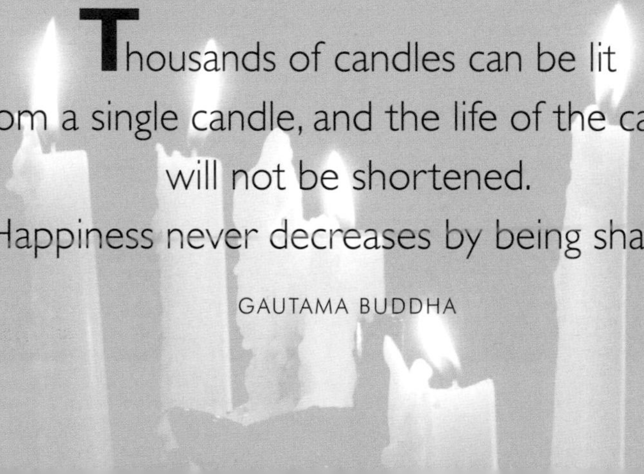

Thousands of candles can be lit
from a single candle, and the life of the candle
will not be shortened.
Happiness never decreases by being shared.

GAUTAMA BUDDHA

Do more of what makes you happy...

Let yourself
be silently drawn
by the strange
pull of what you
really love.
It will not lead
you astray.

JALAL AL-DIN MUHAMMAD RUMI

Do more of what makes you happy...

A happy life is
founded on love
and friendship.
It is guided
by honesty
and integrity.

STUART & LINDA MACFARLANE

Do more of what makes you happy...

JUNE 3

THE GREATEST WEALTH IS CONTENTMENT WITH A LITTLE.

PROVERB

Do more of what makes you happy...

AUGUST 1

We are constituted so that simple acts of kindness such as giving to charity or expressing gratitude, have a positive effect on our long-term moods. The key to the happy life, it seems, is the good life, a life with sustained relationships, challenging work and connections to community.

PAUL BLOOM

Do more of what makes you happy...

JUNE 4

With freedom, books, flowers and the moon, who could not be happy?

OSCAR WILDE

Do more of what makes you happy...

JULY 31

To awaken each morning with a smile brightening my face;
to greet the day with reverence for the opportunities it contains;
to approach my work with a clean mind;
to hold ever before me, even in the doing of little things,
the ultimate purpose toward which I am working; to meet men
and women with laughter on my lips and love in my heart;
to be gentle, kind, and courteous through all the hours;
to approach the night with weariness that ever woos sleep
and the joy that comes from work well done –
this is how I desire to waste wisely my days.

THOMAS DEKKER

Do more of what makes you happy...

JUNE 5

Scientists believe that having
and caring for house plants
can be very beneficial to our health.
Having plants around us can reduce
stress levels, boost mood
and improve concentration. Further
studies may reveal why, but it is thought
that the act of caring for plants
is therapeutic... and of course we all love
to be surrounded by nature's beauty.

BRIAN CLYDE

Do more of what makes you happy...

Everyone knows a joy shared is a joy doubled.
So share your happiness.
It's really not that complicated.
Share your good news with everyone.

DALTON EXLEY

Do more of what makes you happy...

JUNE 6

Be kind to your future self.
Overspending now will cause unhappiness
to your future self. Neglecting your health now
will result in problems for your future self.
Failure to cherish family and friends
will result in sorrow for your future self.
Live your life in such a way that you can be happy now
without it causing you regrets in the years to come.

STUART & LINDA MACFARLANE

Do more of what makes you happy...

Keep love in your heart. A life without it is like
a sunless garden when the flowers are dead.
The consciousness of loving and being loved brings a warmth
and richness to life that nothing else can bring.

OSCAR WILDE

Do more of what makes you happy...

JUNE 7

My advice is:
Go outside, to the fields, enjoy nature
and the sunshine, go out and try
to recapture happiness...

ANNE FRANK

Do more of what makes you happy...

JULY 28

ANYONE
WHO MASTERS
THE GREY
EVERYDAY
IS A HERO.

FYODOR MIKHAILOVICH
DOSTOYEVSKY

Do more of what makes you happy...

Many persons have a wrong idea of what constitutes true happiness. It is not attained through self-gratification but through fidelity to a worthy purpose.

HELEN KELLER (BORN BOTH DEAF AND BLIND)

Do more of what makes you happy...

JULY 27

We all have people on our "Contact Lists" to whom we haven't spoken for years. Work your way through your list calling each one for a chat and a catch-up. It's good to talk — it's such a therapeutic thing to do.
And it's a fact of life — no one can have too many friends.

BRIAN CLYDE

Do more of what makes you happy...

JUNE 9

Happiness is yours in all nature…
in fields of wildflowers and silent deep forests,
in the mystical mountains, and the song of a distant bird.

SUSAN SQUELLATI FLORENCE

Do more of what makes you happy...

Happiness
is an attitude.
We either make
ourselves miserable,
or happy and strong.
The amount of work
is the same.

FRANCESCA REIGLER

Do more of what makes you happy...

Happiness is knowing you're held in someone's love.

PAMELA DUGDALE

Do more of what makes you happy...

...if only I knew when I was younger how possible things are... if I had only known the difference between happiness and unhappiness is purely confidence.

BERYL BAINBRIDGE

Do more of what makes you happy...

What does it take to be happy?
Wealth? It may help but there are plenty of miserable
rich people. Power? Used for the good it would help
you be happy but more often it just brings stress.
Beauty? No... probably not. Attitude is
what makes you happy; a determination
to find good in all situations and not to despair
when there are setbacks. Develop a positive attitude
and make happiness a priority in your life.

LINDA GIBSON

Do more of what makes you happy...

JULY 24

Our great strength is not in never
feeling sad but in learning from those times of sadness
and using them to enhance our happiness.

LINDA MACFARLANE

Do more of what makes you happy...

JUNE 12

When you go to a garden
do you look at the weeds? Spend more time
with the roses and jasmines.

JALAL AL-DIN MUHAMMAD RUMI

Do more of what makes you happy...

JULY 23

One of the things I keep learning
is that the secret of being happy is doing things
for other people.

DICK GREGORY

Do more of what makes you happy...

Avoid greatness; in a cottage there may be more real happiness than kings or the nobility enjoy.

HORACE

Do more of what makes you happy...

Do we need to make a special effort to enjoy
the beauty of the blue sky? Do we have to practice
to be able to enjoy it? No, we just enjoy it. Each second,
each minute of our lives can be like this.
Wherever we are, any time, we have the capacity
to enjoy the sunshine, the presence of each other,
even the sensation of our breathing.
We don't have to travel into the future to enjoy our breathing.
We can be in touch with these things right now.

THICH NHAT HANH

Do more of what makes you happy...

JUNE 14

So many people discontented with their life think
if they only had what they don't they'd be happy. Sadly it doesn't
tend to work that way. You can be happy with very little,
it's not what you have or don't, it's how you see life.

DALTON EXLEY

Do more of what makes you happy...

To know the reach of one's abilities,
to strive and to achieve that reach,
this is happiness.

PEARL S. BUCK

Do more of what makes you happy...

DETERMINE
TO LIVE LIFE
WITH FLAIR
AND LAUGHTER.

MAYA ANGELOU

Do more of what makes you happy...

JULY 20

JOY EXISTS
ONLY IN
SELF-ACCEPTANCE.
SEEK PERFECT
ACCEPTANCE,
NOT A PERFECT LIFE.

AUTHOR UNKNOWN

Do more of what makes you happy...

If you have time to spare, volunteer to help others,
or help run a sporting event such as a park run.
Helping others, while being part of a team,
is not only a joy but makes an extremely worthwhile
contribution to society.

BRIAN CLYDE

Do more of what makes you happy...

JULY 19

Happiness is a thing of care and consideration,
it's everywhere. The birds and the bees show
happiness to the trees. The sea and the water show care
to the creatures in it. Happiness dominates disaster.
It glooms away the sorrows which hang among swallows.
Happiness is a world of pleasure.
Happiness just comes and goes like the wild things.
It's gone now but it will be back.

J. QUINNEY

Do more of what makes you happy...

JUNE 17

It is worth thousands of pounds a year
to have the habit of looking on the bright side of things.

DR. SAMUEL JOHNSON

Do more of what makes you happy...

The certainty of miserableness
is much safer than
the riskiness of happiness.
So let's all be miserable
for ninety per cent of the day then?
No, let's risk happiness.
What do we have to lose?
Miserableness? Precisely.

DALTON EXLEY

Do more of what makes you happy...

JUNE 18

Don't dream
that broken dream,
don't let sorrow crush your soul.
Dream of love, dream of life,
don't dream
that broken dream,
let happiness be your goal.

STUART & LINDA MACFARLANE

Do more of what makes you happy...

Take off your watch.
Time is meaningless.
Do not try to measure it.
Do not try to control it.
Live in this moment.
Laugh in this moment.
Love in this moment.
It is too precious to be wasted.

LINDA GIBSON

Do more of what makes you happy...

JUNE 19

Happiness never lasts
when it's based
on controlling the world
and others, because
we change and the world
changes and there is nothing
we can do about it.

FARIS BADAWI

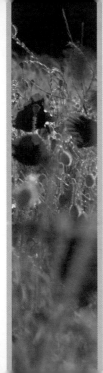

Do more of what makes you happy...

JULY 16

Every day, think
as you wake up:
Today I am fortunate
to have woken up.
I am alive. I have
a precious human life.
I am not going to waste it.

MAHAYANA BUDDHIST QUOTATION

Do more of what makes you happy...

JUNE 20

Happiness waits for us
in unexpected places.
A sudden swirl of starlings.
A picture in the corner
of some gallery.
A busker in the street.
A conversation in a bus queue.
A meteor shower.

PAMELA DUGDALE

Do more of what makes you happy...

JULY 15

ONLY A LIFE LIVED FOR OTHERS IS WORTH LIVING.

ALBERT EINSTEIN

Do more of what makes you happy...

JUNE 21

The first thing
to be done
is laughter,
because that sets
the trend
for the whole day.

OSHO

Do more of what makes you happy...

JULY 14

What is happiness? It is to accept all that
comes into our lives for good or ill.
It is to develop a love of one's employment,
however humble... to realise the gift of laughter...
to know where to go for courage in adversity...
It is to cherish the confidence of friends,
ever conscious of their needs...

EDITOR "GRACE" MAGAZINE

Do more of what makes you happy...

JUNE 22

FIND HAPPINESS IN A QUIET, PERPETUAL REJOICING IN SMALL EVENTS.

HANNAH C. KLEIN

Do more of what makes you happy...

JULY 13

The shock of failure, of disappointments,
of betrayal, hits like a physical blow.
Breathless and blinded, you lose
all contact with the life you lived till now –
the ordinary life that seemed untouchable.
Hold fast. However impossible it seems
that happiness and certainty will return
– they will, they will…

PAM BROWN

Do more of what makes you happy...

JUNE 23

Remember the story
of the old man who on his deathbed said
he'd had a lot of trouble in his life,
most of which had never happened.
A lifetime is all too brief
a moment in time.
Just be. Just be happy.

DALTON EXLEY

Do more of what makes you happy...

JULY 12

Always have something enjoyable to look forward to;
a holiday, a trip to a museum, lunch with a friend.
When you are feeling tired and low,
think about the nice things that you have got arranged.

LINDA GIBSON

Do more of what makes you happy...

JUNE 24

They are wise who
do not grieve
for the things
which they don't have,
but rejoice for those
which they have.

EPICTETUS

Do more of what makes you happy...

LIFE IS A GREAT BIG CANVAS; THROW ALL THE PAINT ON IT YOU CAN.

DANNY KAYE

Do more of what makes you happy...

JUNE 25

Happiness is a butterfly which, when pursued,
is always just beyond your grasp,
but which, if you sit down quietly, may alight upon you.

NATHANIEL HAWTHORNE

Do more of what makes you happy...

All real and wholesome enjoyments possible to us
have been just as possible to us, since
first we were made of the earth, as they are now:
and they are possible to us chiefly in peace.
To watch the corn grow, and the blossoms set;
to draw hard breath over ploughshare or spade;
to read, to think, to love, to hope, to pray –
these are the things that make people happy.

JOHN RUSKIN

Do more of what makes you happy...

JUNE 26

All the joy the world contains
has come from wishing
happiness for others.
All the misery the world contains
has come through wanting
pleasure for oneself.

SHANTIDEVA

Do more of what makes you happy...

JULY 9

Laughing stirs up the blood, expands the chest, electrifies the nerves, clears away the cobwebs from the brain, and gives the whole system a cleansing rehabilitation.

AUTHOR UNKNOWN

Do more of what makes you happy...

JUNE 27

What a fine lesson is conveyed to the mind,
to watch only for the smiles and neglect the frowns of fate,
to compose our lives of bright and gentle moments,
turning always to the sunny side of things, and letting the rest
slip from our imaginations, unheeded or forgotten.

WILLIAM HAZLITT

Do more of what makes you happy...

Happiness does not come automatically.
It is not a gift that good fortune bestows upon us
and a reversal of fortune takes back.
It depends on us alone. One does not become happy
overnight, but with patient labour, day after day.
Happiness is constructed, and that requires effort and time.
In order to become happy, we have to learn
how to change ourselves.

LUCA AND FRANCESCO CAVALLI-SFORZA

Do more of what makes you happy...

JUNE 28

The reality that is present to us and in us:
call it being… silence. And the simple fact that
by being attentive, by learning to listen
(or recovering the natural capacity to listen)
we can find ourself engulfed in such happiness
of being at one with everything in that hidden ground
of Love for which there can be no explanations…
may we all grow in grace and peace, and
not neglect the silence that is printed in the centre
of our being. It will not fail us.

THOMAS MERTON

Do more of what makes you happy...

To have enough is happiness,
to have more than enough is harmful.
That is true of all things, but especially of money.

LAO TZU

Do more of what makes you happy...

JUNE 29

Learn to take a little time –
even if it is a moment in the garden, a gallery, a café.
Appreciate it. Let birds and frogs and pictures, music and books
and undemanding friends heal you.

PAM BROWN

Do more of what makes you happy...

JULY 6

There are
three simple steps
to happiness:
1) Smile
2) Smile
3) Smile

STUART & LINDA MACFARLANE

Do more of what makes you happy...

JUNE 30

The best remedy for those
who are afraid, lonely, or unhappy
is to go outside, somewhere where
they can be quiet. As long as
this exists, and it certainly always will,
then there will always be comfort
for every sorrow,
whatever the circumstances may be.

ANNE FRANK

Do more of what makes you happy...

Research shows that laughter causes
the same increase in blood flow as aerobic exercise –
so forget the treadmill and put on a funny DVD.

BRIAN CLYDE

Do more of what makes you happy...

JULY 1

ONE TODAY IS WORTH TWO TOMORROWS.

BENJAMIN FRANKLIN

Do more of what makes you happy...

JULY 4

Listen to the music you love.
Surround yourself with
things that make you feel spoiled.
Love life! Be happy!

PAMELA DUGDALE

Do more of what makes you happy...

JULY 2

Be happy in small things.
They give great happinesses the opportunity
to creep up on you, quietly.

PAM BROWN

Do more of what makes you happy...

Happiness comes when
we forget about it and become absorbed in
what we do – helping others, working hard,
developing a skill. In none of them are
we looking for happiness, but you can be sure
that if it is there we shall find it.

FROM "THE FRIENDSHIP BOOK OF FRANCIS GAY"